MW01698224

Triple No. 9

Rufo Quintavalle
J.R. Solonche
Bryson Newhart

The Ravenna Triple Series

Chapbooks as they were meant to be read—
in good company.

ISBN: 978-1-7326416-6-2

Published by Ravenna Press
USA
ravennapress.com

FIRST EDITION

Rufo Quintavalle

Rain Songs

Contents

A week, a year, whatever

i.

So many
have
started

out from silence
but I will start
from
something else

like

maybe the sprawl
of this afternoon.

ii.

After all
it really
has everything
in it:
a tree, some noise
of cars

and not
              so long ago
lunch.

iii.

For the longest time

I worried
                  people
would come
                    up over

the wall
                and
get me
              but I don't

worry about that

anymore

even as I speak

a column of silica
is blowing over

Europe
          and all that
seems to matter
                    are
the cancelled flights

I'm not even sure
this goal
             getting
the point
            of view

which would be
truly
        detached
from
        our own

self-interest
                  is
desirable
            but still
from time
            to time

I wish we'd try

always to deny

the angelic
                    in
our nature
                  seems
to be
          the only role

someone decided
to leave the poets

well
            whoever they
were
            I never met
them
          and their dicta

carry small weight
with me

no, I think
                  the wall
will hold
                 just fine
and if
            it doesn't

let them
come.

iv.

In the street
it is

time for
the children

to be picked up
from school
they
will all go
home
or more
likely

(it is sunny
today

like it hasn't
been
in weeks)

to a park

but one of the
boys
is crying.

v.

This funny thing

happened
then
I went
up
on
the roof
and a
strong wind
picked up
just as

the restaurant

switched off
their
extractor fan

so one sound

stopped
            when
the other
               began

and the wind

carried off
the cooking smells

and

       tossed them
with
        the cumulus.

vi.

So you see, there really is everything.

Figs

The city is cold but somewhere figs
swell in an October sun.

Today the huge idea of money stopped
but the force which makes money gather and burst,
which used to move through God
and some say will again,
will outlive money itself.

Because things are
they have a preference for life,
and we call good whatever lets them grow.

Like wind on a field

At night
a plane

one big idea

like wind
on
a field

makes
all the windows
buzz

a child
screams, falls back
to sleep

a hedgehog
moves
its thousand
spikes.

Much

Because
little
is true
beyond
its own
terms we
assume
nothing
can be
surely
known so
that that
self same
nothing
becomes
both end
(that is
failing)
and end
(that is
summum)
of thought;
but since
little
exists
outside

its own
terms this
self same
nothing
is not
only
only
sometimes
true but
also
when it
is is

Static

In half-lit rooms a radio tuned to nothing buzzes static,
a burr like the music of history,

which explains nothing
but without which we cannot explain;

it is this sound not silence we wake and sleep to
and by it know we are the same that wake who slept.

Theories of Justice

It was after glue had been poured on the town
then lifted off like a gummy negative
that the folk went naked through the naked streets
to test the persistence of law in a world
where daylight showed no tact or history,
their shoulder blades, haunches and genital scraps
advancing in silence past the sandstone walls.

The bugs

The bugs are in the bedroom,
  the bugs are in my mind;

The bugs were there before us,
  the bugs and their ilk
  will outlast time;

The bugs are in the food we eat,
  the bugs are in my gut;

E coli pluribus unum:
  without the bugs
  there is no us.

The ruins of the ruins of palmyra

plasma, map, soup, her, yet, so, soapy,
prism, mish mash, rope, she, sheet, rip,
hirsute, hurt, shiny, ship shape, heresy,
silt, least, salt, thrall, enthrall, hunters,
shout, hoist, throat, into, paste, of, yeti,
parse, the, runes, then, faint, in, history,
onto, sin, noise, heroin, mute, ratio, oar,
ear, rather, one, true, truth, islam, salami,
asylum, prison, poise, foist, roister, slip,
pin up, poison, reason, moral, aneurism,
amateur, heather, psyllium, surly, foal, if,
horse, play, happily, after, all, fire, heifer,
shutter, homes, plan, earlier, lately, hut,
a, youth, pops, holy, photos, fun, house

The night it rained

The night it rained
three weeks
in half an hour
the rain fell
on us
and washed
away the streets,
and we all
kept on drinking
as if it was
Weimar.

Rain song

There are
no origins,
only now

an afternoon
downpour
followed by
light

wet rocks
in sun,
a sodden
hibiscus

and it is
in surpassing
our
sacred
texts

that we are true
to them
and faithful.

Because the night

Because the night
surrounds us,
because the cold
has got up
through our feet,
because the street
curves gently,
because in the dark
neon and an odor
of felt, because
the cellar door,
because the night,
despite the heart's
imperative, thins,
because the distant
sky, the stairwell,
because the boat,
the shifty moon,
because the pollen
is a dusty glove
on tarmac, because
the crab is inside
out, because want
warmth, comfort
despair, hessian
and a smell of clay

in rain, because,
despite it all,
a pillow, despite
the streetlights
sleep, despite
the jackhammers
dawn, because
the night, because
the hell of appetite,
because the damp
sand on an empty
beach, because
a quickening, as if
that were enough,
is enough, because,
despite it all,
a lumbering sound,
an odor of fat
on the foggy air,
smoke, the smell
of cows, of grass,
of prehistoric
ferns, because,
despite it all,
a moon like
a membrane, rubber
valve through which
the weather comes,
because the cold,

because the pull
of underearth,
because the endless
weather, because,
despite it all
despite it all
the weather.

The well

And so
you go back
to the well

not
because
you
want to
but
because
you thirst;

character
they say is
fate

but today
I woke
in sunlight
trembling

ants
on the table
were eating
a wasp
I had

almost
gone

almost
to the end
of my
mistake

Place du Carrousel

The president passes in a motorcade;
let him pass.

The sun is kissing my eyes
and I know I shall never go hungry.

Rocks

If this is all there is
then I can live with that
(time that is
and the way it goes too quick)
but if it is not,
if there is more
(and when they say more
they mean much more)
then I do not see
how one can own this fact,
that we come to the light
like rocks in a plot of land
and have no choice
and will not cease to be,
and live.

Speech to silence

If all explaining
is explaining away

and telling merely
telling tales

I still will
favor speech

to silence;

truth is out there
is a thing

and briefly
we inhabit it

One body

But in as much as we all
    have one heart, matching limbs
    and a brain-gut axis

aren't we all, to some degree
    little c conservatives
    who fight our corner,
    move through space

and want, deep down, to know
    what is for lunch;

starch and beans, a little
    fat, that which unites us,
    humanity, schmaltz.

The grass

Once when we walked forever in the grass
and the sky was open like a beggar's smile;

once when the others told us a lie,
and told us the rivers and fields were signs;

and once for those we cannot save,
the angels for whom the world is too much.

Well, here I am

Well, here I am with all of my love
  and all of my anger
                    and all my mistakes

a heavy boat manoeuvres up the Schelde,
and the wind slams shut the bedroom door

a little inland, pollen in clouds
shifts like a dynasty
                              moves over land

& I have no landscape
                     save the landscape

within
   my mind   its better eye

lighting our house like sun in Hong Kong smog;

my kids like the creature
                                      resent their birth

they will hold it against existence forever
a slanting house in an orderly terrace

and all ingenuity
turned towards war

to the putting asunder of what was once one;

a gust of wind blows open the window
and then slams shut the bedroom door.

The Jewish Dancing Master

J.R. Solonche

Contents

The Jewish Dancing Master

I teach ladies and gentlemen to dance
because I dance well.
I am an excellent dancer.

My first love, however, is singing.
But my singing voice is poor.
I do not sing at all well.

I am an excellent dancer,
so my feet carry my tune.
My feet are my very excellent voice.

Halleluiah! Halleluiah!
Alas. Alas. Alas.

Namesake

Three chapters.
Seventy-three verses.

Longer than that of Haggai.
But what son is named Haggai?

Longer than that of Habakkuk.
But what son is named Habakkuk?

Longer than that of Zephariah.
But what son is named Zephariah?

Three chapters.
Seventy-three verses.

He wrote so little, this Joel,
This minor prophet of the Old Testament.

He wrote so little, this Joel.
Does anybody know anything about him, this Joel?

I for one know nothing of him.
And I of all people should know of him.

I who am named for him
should know all there is of the man whose name he has.

Three chapters only.
Seventy-three verses only.

So he must not have been a professional, this Joel.
As was Isaiah who said sixty-six chapters.

As was Jeremiah who said fifty-two chapters.
As was Ezekiel who said forty-eight chapters.

It is obvious this Joel was a part time prophet only.
It is obvious he did not support himself with
prophesying.

He must have practiced a trade, this Joel, this minor
prophet.
He must have been a shepherd, or a potter of pots.

He must have been a scribe, or a weaver of cloth.
He must have been a vinedresser, or a mender of tents.

You wrote so little, Joel.
O, minor prophet of concise consternation.

Ellis Island

Steamer trunks, carpet bags,
wicker baskets with leather straps,
hair brushes, combs, lacey handkerchiefs,
bibles, jewelry, beer mugs, bowls,
straight razors, razor strops, hat pins,
hats, shoes, vests, a violin, a certificate
of piano studies, identity papers, shawls,
my father, aged thirteen, on the stern
of the S.S. Rotterdam, looking back
at the sea… at the sea… at the sea…

The Stories

Once there were 10,000 people on Orchard Street.
Once there were 10,000 people on Rivington Street.
There could have been many stories.
Or there could have been one story told many times
over.
Were there 10,000 stories on Orchard Street?
Were there 10,000 stories on Rivington Street?
Or was there one story on Orchard Street told 10,000
times over?
Or was there one story on Rivington Street told 10,000
times over?

Morris Karp

Morris Karp was born in Russia.
Morris Karp was the father of my mother.
Morris Karp came to America in 1910.

Morris Karp spoke only Russian.
Morris Karp learned English in America.
Morris Karp got a job operating a sewing machine in
America.

Morris Karp made pockets for businessmen's jackets in
America.
Morris Karp made pockets for businessmen's coats in
America.
Morris Karp knew injustice in America.

Morris Karp did not know the word *injustice.*
Morris Karp was active in the union of garment workers.
Morris Karp fought for a 40-hour week.

Morris Karp fought for decent conditions of work.
Morris Karp fought for a living wage.
Morris Karp was beaten by a police officer on the street.

Morris Karp showed me the scar he got in America.
Morris Karp showed me the perfect pockets he made
for businessmen in America.
Morris Karp told me something.

Morris Karp told me how he learned the difference
between *tear* and *tear.*
Morris Karp said, *A tear is a tear in your eye.*
Morris Karp said, *A tear is a tear in your pocket.*

High Holy Days

I remember in synagogue more than
a sin ago, the portion of the torah
always the same, the story of Jonah,
the whale and God's demands,

the men and my father in their milky
prayer shawls, the old ones yellowed
with years and sputum stained, bowed
and bent back and forth, the silky

strings at both ends splashing the oaken
bench in front of us like ocean foam.
How seasick I was among them
as I mumbled under my broken

breathing, under that noise, that wish –
Leave him alone … Leave me alone …
Atone … Atone … Alone …
the wash of surf on a stony beach.

The Jonah Story

I do not like the Jonah story. The Jonah story is all obedience and disobedience,
God calling on the wind to frighten the sailors, God calling on the whale
to swallow up Jonah and spit him out again on dry land, God calling on the worm
to desolate the vine. The Jonah story is all God calling. I do not like the way
the Jonah story ends. The Jonah story ends without ending. It ends with God asking
Jonah a question, but really asking one of those holy rhetorical questions that God is
so fond of, and that is where Jonah is left hanging, on the question mark of God.
And I do not like this because I want to know what happens to heroes at the end of stories.
What happens to Jonah at the end of his story? What does Jonah do? Does he go home?
Does he stay where he is on the east side of Nineveh where he prepares a field

of gourd vines? Does he sleep twenty-four hours
through? Does God leave Jonah alone?
Does God leave Jonah alone, finally, oh finally, in the
shade of the vine?

The Guide of the Perplexed

When I was nineteen or twenty,
I started to read
"The Guide of the Perplexed"
by Moses Maimonides.
I was nineteen or twenty.
I was perplexed.
I needed a guide.
I read a few pages.
Perhaps I read a chapter.
I don't remember.
But I soon realized I needed a guide to the guide.
I have never gone back to read more
of "The Guide of the Perplexed"
by Moses Maimonides.
He should have illustrated
the text with pictures of roses. Or
daisies.

Diary of 56 Days in an Israeli Psychiatric Hospital

And on the first day
they stared at him as he shaved and he showered

And on the second day
one introduced himself to him
and he had scars on both wrists
and they stared at him as he shaved and he showered
and they gave him bitter cigarettes
and they gave him breakfast

And on the third day
he taught himself
to smoke the bitter cigarettes
they gave him before breakfast
and the one with scars on both wrists
showed him the rope-burn on his throat
and they stared at him as he shaved and as he showered

And on the fourth day
another one introduced himself
and he asked him for a bitter cigarette

and he had skin like goat's milk and eyes like the blue sky
and he asked him if he were an angel
and he said that yes he was
and he asked him if he would fly for him
and he said that yes he would
and they stared at him as he shaved and as he showered

And on the fifth day
he played chess with a Polish poet and lost
and at noon he flew for the one
with the skin like goat's milk and the eyes like the sky
and when he came back to earth
he asked him for three bitter cigarettes
and they stared at him as he shaved and as he showered

And on the sixth day
the one with the scars on both wrists
and the rope-burn on his throat
showed him a picture of his mother
and for some reason they no longer stared at him as he
shaved and as he showered

And on the seventh day
the one with skin like goat's milk and eyes like the sky

asked him for all his bitter cigarettes
and the one with scars on both wrists
and a rope-burn on his throat and the picture of his
  mother
asked him to teach him how to fly
and he said that yes he would
he would teach him how to fly
for all his bitter cigarettes

Walk around the room seven times
and seven times chant the foregoing

Prayer for a Friend Who Has Probably Committed Suicide

I cannot pray until I remember.
So I remember our first meeting in the vestibule of
   hospital.
I was playing chess.
You were holding a paper sack and stood behind me,
   not speaking a word.
After I was mated, you spoke in English.
When I asked how you knew, you shrugged.

I cannot pray until I remember.
So I remember your basement room in Haifa.
You showed me the reviews: "Most talented...Another
   Chagall..."
And the photograph of you dancing with Margot
   Fonteyn.
You offered me coffee in the cup you used for cleaning
   palette knives.
You looked at me and shrugged.

I cannot pray until I remember.
So I remember the rule that every ass had to be painted.
Every ass had to be posed like a peach.
One was a woman on a beach whose face was an ass.
Next to the woman was a fish with your face.
Above you the moon, which was made of goatskin.
You said it was called "Waiting for Bardot," and
shrugged.

I cannot pray until I remember.
So I remember that day in the cafe on the Carmel.
You stood on the chair and waved your arms like a wild
man.
You were trying to throw your hands away.
You were cursing your hands.
You were naming your ten fingers for the ten plagues of
Egypt.
You were naming one finger for one plague.
When you were done, you shrugged.
Damn you, you shrugged.

Dreams in Eden

1. *Adam's Dream*

First there was this strange sensation
like a finger running along my ribs.
It was quick, firm, with neither pleasure nor pain.
Then I was lying on my back.
A great tree took root between my legs.
In a moment it grew to its full height.
It swayed in the wind.
Then it exploded into a glorious crown of fruit.
An angel of the Lord came with a flaming sword.
The angel of the Lord burned the tree to ashes.
I scooped the ashes up into the cup of my hands.
I rubbed the ashes into the skin of my chest and
   shoulders.
I rubbed the ashes into the skin of my arms and legs.
I found myself in a new place.
Behind me I heard laughter and weeping.
I heard laughter and weeping near me.

2. *Eve's Dream*

I dreamed I was being dreamed.
In the beginning, I was a flower.
My face opened to the sun.
I breathed without taking breaths.
Then I stretched my body and found
more of my body. My fingers, my hands,
my arms moved. I became a butterfly.
I shivered in the warm air.
But my body ended at the waist.
Only later did my hips appear.
And then my thighs and my legs.
I could not wait any longer.
I became a gazelle.
I kicked free and leaped clear.
The air was fragrant with grass.
I leaned against an apple tree,
standing on only my hind legs.
I awakened him with a touch.

3. *Short Speech for Adam*

When I awoke from
that deep sleep, I saw her there,
nearby,
in the shade of two trees.
Her hands were on her hips
and she was speaking to me
in the language of the hyenas.

Isaac to Abraham

You never asked me if I was afraid.
Was that because you were afraid?
Afterward, because I had fainted
from fear, I woke up and smelled
the smoke of the sacrifice. The ram
was charred black and the smoke
sickened me and I felt like
fainting again but you held me up.
You were weeping from joy. You said
God had only tested you. You said God
had set the ram in the thicket to be burned
as sacrifice instead of me. But you never
asked if I was afraid. Was that because
you were afraid? I wanted to tell you
I was afraid. I wanted to tell you I was sick
from the smoke and I felt like fainting again.
I wanted to tell you I was afraid that God
would change His mind and send the angel
back again to tell you I was the sacrifice again.
I was sick from the smoke but I did not want
you to be ashamed of me. Every night

I have the same dream. The angel of the Lord comes and says, “Isaac, wake your son!”

Jacob and the Angel

Afterward in the morning,
already late in the morning,
already near noon,
he awoke,
and no one was about.
His right hand was gripped tightly
on the shin of his leg.
His left arm was under his head
so that the elbow was stiff,
and the forearm was numb
from the weight of his head upon it.
His mouth was dry with the dryness of sand,
and the lips of his mouth were parched as the sand of
the desert.
He felt the soreness in his limbs.
He felt the stiffness in the joints of his limbs.
He saw the full light of day illuminating the tent.
The flap of the tent opening was bright with the
brightness of daylight.
And even full with soreness in his body,
and even full with stiffness in his limbs,

and even full with a terrible thirst in his mouth, he sprang to his feet,
and he threw himself upon the tent opening,
upon the full light of the tent opening, that flapped like big, white wings.

Poem for Franz Kafka on his Birthday

Franz, virtuoso of guilt,
Franz, master craftsman of ambivalence,
Franz, lover of the dark haired beauty, introspection,
and of her younger fair haired sister, paralysis,

Franz, not to you do I extend a wish,
but from you do I ask a wish today.

Franz, as only K could, as only K would,
tell me please in two hundred pages of crystalline
German,
how many ways I could say *Happy Birthday*
to one who wished he'd never been born?

False Messiah

We have stopped
the full-page ads
in the newspaper
and taken his picture

down from the signs
in Brooklyn.
We have cancelled
the charters to the Holy Land.

We have shorn our side-locks
and rent our cassocks.
We have sanctified our kitchens
and shut in our women.

We have ordered new ink,
new paper, new books.
We have told the carpenters
to measure oak for new chairs.

We have screwed new bulbs tight
into the sockets of our lights
and begged our children
for their forgiveness. Amen.

Often I Wonder

Often I wonder
what I would have done
had I been there.
Would I have tried to run
through the back of the house
or leaped out of a window
or hidden in the coal bin?
Would I have fought with them
and been killed right there
on the step of the front door,
right then in the middle of the night?
Would I have gone obediently
without a murmur?
And at the station later,
would I have grabbed under an arm for a gun
hoping to take at least one?
And later in the cattle-wagon,
would I have cut open a vein
in my wrist with the glass of my glasses
I would have broken?
And later, in the camp,

would I have starved myself, given
my bread to another?
I never wonder if I would have lived.
That would be a sin.

Jehova's Witnesses

They also suffered.
They also died by the thousands in the camps.
They too were man's witnesses, these Jehovah's
witnesses.
They too were murdered, and when they come to my
door,
as this morning, a married couple, or two women and a
child,
well-dressed, in a car just waxed, gleaming in the
sunlight,
soft-spoken, smiling, sincere in everything, rehearsed
by the elders, I want to talk to them about suffering and
witness,
but all they want to talk about is Jehovah,
and his plan for the world, and his plan for me,
and why they alone are right. They alone.

The Last Survivor

In a nursing home in Tel Aviv,
in twenty years, they will find him
wearing a yellow bathrobe.
He will be one hundred and five.

The number on his arm will not be clear
enough to read, a blur, a purple bruise.
He will be blind and nearly deaf.
They will shout questions in his ear.

Each answer will be a dry twig's crack.
"These Mengele, they were Jews?"
"I saw many, a thousand, a million."
"It was gray, it was white, it was black."

"One a week a cigar. One a day a schnapps."
The nurse will wave them away.
"Time for his afternoon nap."
And he will die peacefully the next day.

Bryson Newhart

Werza

Part 1: Note from a Retired Entertainer

In the last years of pendulous battle, I entertained soldiers as a highwire walker, working just below the procreators that performed on a higher rope. They were the people from whom we'd all been spawned, and on a non-obscure day, squinting at the sun through my field glasses, I could sometimes see a face that resembled my own.

Wers were a strange mix of business, entertainment, and conflict. Wers were something that nobody understood. They were shown on television so I'm not sure why. The pendulous battles took place inside a dome or head, and were conducted in the air as entertainments guaranteeing our security, but which, as entertainments, required further entertainments; hence, the spectacle of our volant lives.

Unlike soldiers who never left the domes, our first job was to return to the homeland on an airship. There we made weapons and learned to walk the rope, and at a certain age we were stuffed into coffins. The coffins were mailed back to the remote locations where the battles were filmed to boost soldier moral, to make light of the darkness and darkness of the light. Wer was a serious business that was shown on television, although it was not just shown on television. I'm not sure why. It was part of a huge industry.

Our nation's soldiers were strung up by their ankles, miles above the earth. They had been borne for this purpose; just as we had been borne for our own purpose. Part of their job, like us, was to bounce above the earth on bungee cords.

Enter the air clowns, always fresh from the homeland, our amusing lives always at stake. To entertain the soldiers we jumped from the coffins. Often the roles were blurred just as blood became blurry in the sky, and thus it was almost impossible to distinguish us, not only from each other, but from the actual soldiers. We wore the same uniforms and carried guns. We were often enlisted as bafs to perform beside volant soldiers in pendulous flight.

Among the most popular entertainers were the toddlers, delivered at birth by General Goodwrench, a thin figure posing stiffly on the wire with his tools. This periodic ritual of spawning was conducted by General Goodwrench and helped to remind soldiers of religion, of whatever their ligaments led back to, the interior of their bones or lands of origin, places they had never seen.

Children such as myself became hysterical entertainment soldiers whose bodies grew into uniforms designed for entertainment, and who learned to make weapons while learning to walk the ropes. I'm not exactly sure who won those wers. I don't think anyone knows that.

Part 2: Message from Earth

Because we do not understand you, Gosper has proposed that we describe our ways—our wers. Soon there will be nothing left of us, so to communicate the complexity of our world, our ways and wers, we have decided to encapsulate our wers for you, for you who do not know about these things. It is our hope that you will learn our language and become a dog; that you may speak, bark, and become a fighter in the game of life. It is our hope that you may burn while hanging, volant and pendulous on a bungee cord. This is why we are sending you these messages through time and space. If you are reading this, or merely trying to, the capsules have begun to bomb your planet. They have begun to bombard it with the intent of blowing up the spot, thereby destroying peanuts in a jiffy until the work has become a don jaun.

The capsules have begun to send a message. If a hollow piece of plastic filled with messages kills you or a loved one, consider the violence of language. Language allows us to understand one another, enabling us to blow things up, to set flame to things. This, we understand, is the bomb. If you do not agree with us or understand, think about the capsules that may kill you. A dictionary may land on your head and kill you, because you're are not of this world. Such operations occur every minute. For us, utter peace would be the absence of language and consciousness.

Encapsulation: consider that thoughts come from words whose individual meanings are derived by negation, the negation of all other meanings. We know this because the measuring tape told us. Consider, for example, a rock. Let's briefly examine it. It is defined by what it is not. As a weapon, we may say:

A) While a piece of feldspar (metamorphic or plutonic) may remove an eye, or combined with other sticks and stones break a person's bones more effectively, it is not a homeboy or a bit bucket.

B) Thus we know what a rock is.

C) A rock is not a bugle rag or brilliant buzzard.

D) It is not a boffer. Its meaning destroys those things.

E) While the music of a rock may irritate an enemy, or spread its seeds of wer (sometimes as violence upon a person in the form of expressive object language etched on skin, or other types of objects pierced through the ears, nose, or tongue) a rock, by definition, is not a mumblage or a tractor dump.

F) It is not a tick or patch. It destroys those things.

G) It is not an outlaw shark.

H) While groups of rockers may crush their opponents with powerful curved chair legs or lull them to sleep, a rock is not a smoking clover.

I) It is not a golden key.

J) Nor a sword or a peanut.

K) A rock is not a Conway or Pogo.

L) And thus we know what a rock is.

Part 3: Description of a Pendulous Battle (letter from Alpha Charlie) Section A, The Players

High above the earth, beneath a tacit rainbow, and despite the gaze of the volant eye, the threat of the Wild Weasel, we religioned ourselves to bungee cords, intending to sustain hope, to stretch it above the earth as far as possible, as well as low and close to the earth; then high into the blackness of the ether. In the distance were innumerable screams, not from the other fighters doing battle, but from the studio audience, which consisted of heads and scrubs watching TV, not content to read the bible, waiting until we began to flood mugs.

Among our crew was Busted Jaw, Cobra Judy, The Busy Lawyer, Bubble Dancer, Combat Martin, Haystack, The Idealist, Head Dancer, Little Brother, and Sussman.

Gosper and Conway were engaged in the outer planets that week.

Our objectives included Homeslice, The Belted Fighter, Chickenhead, Boss Baller, Bluebird, Captain Save-A-Hoe, Long Legs, Office Boy, Jimmy, Filthy Moe, G-Ride, The Harvest Reaper, Hubba Roc, and Robo Thug. Who could keep track of so many?

Clowns and toddlers were ready to scheme, and the procreators were coupled and prepared to hit skins, transmitting a broadcast of the pendulous battle. One of the hoe's was pregnant and we wondered if there would be a birth that day. The judges for the event were Ron Superior, Senior Stretch, and General Goodwrench.

Part 3: Description of a Pendulous Battle (letter from Alpha Charlie) Section B, Human Energy

During times of wer before a battle, to prevent scurvy and software rot, opposing crews participated in a lavish feast. After registering at the troll booth, they assembled on the desert floor in separate tents inside of which they sat at high tables. They ate while the final preparations for battle were made.

The feasts were conducted by the Feastocrat, who took turns visiting each crew and imparting his nourishing wisdom. Soldiers sat at high tables wearing feast gear. They sat at tables and banged their fish hooks as the servers cold-chucked combat beef onto their plates. Food was brought to the locations in coffins brimming with chop suey and broccoli, cotton candy and duck, raw pelican and peace pheasant. The soldiers gronked live pilot fish, pulling them from their fish bowls with their fish hooks.

"Wer spelled backwards is raw," the Feastocrat would chant. "Which is how we like our meat. Raw and still pulsing with life as we bite into it."

Gesturing agreement with a handwave, Head Dancer might suddenly barf up some bootie crack corn and say, "Word. Pass da hoe cakes!"

The main course was of course beef, served in long ropes of sausage, or wurst, by an invisible man named Daemon. Soldiers dipped it into garlic salt, then chopped it into bits, licking it off their plates and grills. They cleaned away the flavor with their tongues. Chewy batches of liver marinated in gravy were flipped onto their faces (grills), and the prosthetics chonged it together with flakey fried pigeon and frog. Eligible receivers such as The Busy Lawyer were exempt from tableware amd their slop was flipped directly into their mouthpieces. The flavorful, but rare, yu-shiang whole fish was reserved exclusively for such receivers; if a stray goose wandered into the tent, only an eligible receiver had permission to snarf it.

Table status was based on performance in battle and poor performers were rewarded with little food. They were designated as bagbiters and usually given combat apples, or if no battle apples were left, the bags or coffins the apples had come in. Busted Jaw, for example, could usually be seen chipping his corns on a cokebottle, even though he was an excellent performer, or munching on squares of fake ice. Between courses, the soldiers bletched and slurped water, drinking gulps of juice from their money holes.

Grinding, chomping, mashing, crunching, the warriors made their way through the feast, always looking forward to dessert, which consisted of tasty gorp and vanilla fudge, as well as canonical cuban candy and compass cookies. If german chocolate cake was available, it was given to the Idealist, who gobbled it in secret.

"Have donut?" Little Brother might inquire.

Then the Flam Artist would appear and set fire to an edible dummy, providing us with dummy flambé, which was hung from the ceiling in tribute to foo fighters.

Bloated and leaking gasses, the crews found fiery relief in the latrines, flushing their oily waste into the desert in preparation for the armor and weapons inspection.

Part 3: Description of a Pendulous Battle (letter from Alpha Charlie) Section C, Armor and Weapons Inspection

After the feast we left the tents and entered the awaiting bubbles that transported us into the dome, whose walls stretched for miles in all directions. Before the battles could begin we had to pass before the inspectors, Senior Lance, Senior Mace, and Senior Spur, who each wore baldrics and smops, with circlets to keep the hair from their eyes. These gentlemen were responsible for checking our armor flaps and verifying our badges, and assuming things were not in need of frobnicating, they would hand out favors that entitled us to fight. We stood at attention as they inspected our ranks with a duck hook.

First came Cobra Judy, who looked fly in her cobra shoes. She wore a volant dome piece, but little else, and her body was covered with forest-green moondust. She carried a mac and an eight plus one.

"You are an elegant lady," said Senior Mace, putting on his jimmy hat.

He handed one to Senior Spear and they positioned the mirror, then began to claw at Judy's body with duck hooks.

Most of the men wore stunnas and stood at attention waiting for their turn with the hook device. The inspectors worked quickly, checking for gear that was bootsie.

Most soldiers carried light weapons and walking shields, as well as various means for achieving crowd control. They wore hoods and crowns and carried chromes, as well as compasses and combat arrows.

Combat Martin had heavy weapons and a desert shield. He was one of the only soldiers who knew how to use such devices and dragged them behind him on dummy cords. Everyone's garb included dog tags, but Sussman wore a chivalry chain. His iron hand, affixed to a frob, held a compass buffalo.

Another deviation was Busted Jaw, a bama; he prefered heavy chains although they weighed him down, and was crufty in his low goose and khakis, as always rocking the gold tooth. He carried techs, a gat, a chop suey, and a spiked bat, which was more steel than he could handle, causing his form to buckle. Senior Spur pointed this out, that Busted Jaw's persona was a liability, but we weren't ready to kick him off the team because the heads and scrubs loved him, which gave us good ratings. They loved his illegal barking, which he did into a burner and a chip. He was something of an amateur flam artist, one of the few soldiers that got as much attention as the clowns.

Wearing tims and a hard shell, carrying a flaming dart, I waited for my inspection. The bells and whistles sounded and the inspectors moved from soldier to soldier, placing hula hoops around their arms. Combined with the duck hook, the logical hula hoop determined whether or not things were grave.

"Have gold?" an inspector would ask, his silk purse bulging on his belt and a pipe burning in his hirsute mouth.

"Have wedge? Don't front because we can DWIM you. Smell me?"

All of the jocks were stacking, and some of us who did not have hard feddie had to give up our gold ones for a favor. Haystack had forgotten his badge, so they pulled out his gold ones, removing them from his grill with a hook.

As we were ushed into the dome by Senior Lance, I observed the other crew waiting their turn, and I wondered how much grip they'd have to part with. Most of them looked grungy, but they were certainly equipped with gear. For example, Office Boy and Chickenhead were dressed as dragons and carried desert shields and gun-shaped flashlights. Robo Thug had a peace patch and an iron lung. And two of the crew, probably Filthy Moe and Captain Save-A-Hoe, were hidden in speaker and woofer disguises. I bletched, but swallowed it. It was going to be an interesting battle.

Part 3: Description of a Pendulous Battle (letter from Alpha Charlie) Section D, Prelude to Battle

At a handwave from the Autocrat, whose burning vision determined everything from enemy programming to the phases of the moon, each crew was lifted to the ceiling of the dome by Xray Yankee Zulu. Everyone remained in day mode, prepared for the coming drama, and a tacit rainbow met with a white cloud beginning to grow along the edges of the Eric. I wondered if the enemy would make rain or snowflakes, complicating the work of our priests. Given the mounting tail winds this battle was going to be stupid.

Below us, the battle arena was filled with a thousand cords and ropes. Hovering in the center, the volant eye bubbled like a bright star, broadcasting our sheepwalk to the stations. I wondered if Mike November and Uniform Victor were still working the eye as volant ghosts. According to Bubble Dancer, who always fought close to the eye, it was now completely automated; Mike and Victor had been sent to the Moon where they were farmed out as obscure buffalo hunters.

Everyone was tense as Senior Stretch announced the melee rules. Only minor magic would be allowed to be sampled, and everything was kill on sight.

"Probably no rain or snow today," I thought.

Then Senior Stretch surprised everyone and announced that marginal lossage would result in a rollback.

"Your happy weeks of treadmilling are over," he said, striking chords of panic everywhere. "Today there is going to be a sun bath."

The old grind was going to be parsed, and we realized we would all soon die.

I looked at Cobra Judy and she seemed as random as a real user. Not only had she been completely raped by inspection, but she also now looked brain-damaged, her cobra jaws closed and BOE, emoting nothing of the combat angel I seen so many times on a corpse run, surrounded on all sides by flossy cobra mist.

Judy was misfeatured, already broken.

I tried to relax, but everyone was wedged. Bubble Dancer bletched a pilot fish and The Idealist lost his chocolate cake. Little Brother and The Busy Lawyer tried to ignore what we had heard, buzzing about the platform collecting garbage. But things did not look so gravy anymore.

"By the end of this madness the procreators will be spawning a new crews for the Briar Patch," said Sussman.

"Our mugs are flooded," he maved.

Only Busted Jaw seemed in phase, gripping a burner to his corn chamber, his rapper hole busy flaming the audience on its own channel, barking about how he was going aggro. On a bold venture he was going to comb the lists, then go out of pockets and become a Conway. This was probably last minute programming by some powerful hacker, or perhaps Busted Jaw was attempting a Gabriel.

Part 3: Description of a Pendulous Battle (letter from Alpha Charlie) Section E, Battle

There came a second handwave from the Autocrat and the battle began, starting with a series of bombardments that blew up a clown. Before we could dive into the grind, the enemy had opened a hello wall, set fire to several burning dummies, and then boomed into yoyo mode, firing rude bolts into the burning wind. The studio audience cheered and a child was born on the highwire, removed with a hook by General Goodwrench.

Meanwhile, in his flaming woofer disguise now lit by a torch chief, Captain Save-A-Hoe flowed off his bungee, generating a series of heavy beats that punted Haystack off his station and out the frame, straight into a terminal line starve. It was the first KOS of the morning and Sussman wolfed for a chirugeon, shouting "Hold!"

But there wasn't a chirugeon for this battle, as he knew, the melee rules were set for an end game. Hence, the attempted Gabriel was dissed by a bug.

An announcement was made by the Story Teller, saying that god was pleased. It began with the word "wow" and went on to describe how Captain Save-A-Hoe had gone buck wild and hacked the disco lights out of a bum.

Before the cheering fully stopped, Bubble Dancer line-fed himself into the fast lane, where he engaged waving firearms in a deadly embrace with Homeslice and Chickenhead. He flamed both peanuts and performed a long thrust, followed by a tail recursion that murphed Chickenhead and left Homeslice bouncing. Bubble Dancer was off the hook; he had pulled a federal flipper drop, and once the smoke cleared, Story Teller glorked about the features, raising our crews' confidence in the prospect of a freedom train.

But we were not quite getting over, as the party had glitched to algorithmic wheel wers with multiple heads, scrubs, and users in a spirit-rapping frenzy, including the elusive Suitcase Ranger. Everyone was in deadlock, rapping on the highwire just above a team of procreators engaged in birthing a new General Goodwrench. On my own wheel, I battled The Belted Fighter with a flaming dart; he swooped above my head and gave credible chase, one flipper wielding a gat, the other a bible. The Belted Fighter was banging, a foo fighter known for his many skills, but his methods were canonical, and with my gun-shaped flashlight set on a sun run, I was able to feep him into catatonia, then perform a swift tractor dump, achieving the needed kill.

It was a bold venture, and fortunately it helped nerf some of the cons of a very untasty saga taking place on the opposite Eric, where Cobra Judy was battling aggro in the vortex. She faced Hubba Roc and G-Ride and a number of air clowns and priests wearing busted jimmies, and the situation was fugazi: a fencepost error had enabled the enemy to harness enough magic to unleash a cloud—a surprise package that included snow, and which succeeded in snafuing Cobra Judy, trapping her in a tail recursion. Everyone was thrashing her dome, and already her moon dust coating was mixed with random blood that was mostly hers.

It looked grim for Judy, and muttering "bogosity," Sussman began to program a sacred sermon. However, just then Combat Martin and Busted Jaw popped out of the lists. They splattered the enemy with pave paws and bucky bits while I jetted over to serve as the tail chaser, my flashlight on smart mode; together with Martin's heavy weapons and his desert shield swinging around us on dummy cords, and with Busted Jaw's chop suey and spiked bat, we succeeded in restoring a balance of power. The shrieking enemy was sent into a spiraling line starve and I immediately applied fake ice to Judy's bubbling wounds. Not many of us were left by then, but maybe there was still a chance that we might become the chosen ones—the first crew to be granted enduring freedom. If we just continued fighting and did not force the rollback.

But it was too late. God had a plan for us. A final sun bath.

The entertainment below had already left the dome with new crews being spawned for the new programming season, and any second there would be a loud bang and the crash of brilliant pebbles from the moon.

I looked around and soldiers were killing off their features, cutting their ropes and terminating operation in the face of certain death, the coming zero.

They were turning themselves into burning dummies and splatting on the dome floor, releasing gas and waste from corporations.

They would never know how they'd been judged
and neither would I.

◆

Glossary 1: Part 1

ENTERTAINER: Soldier in pendulous battle, believes himself merely entertainer.
BAF: Bring a friend, describes attack of NPC (non-player) or enemy.
BLOOD: A corporation structured by its own incorporation; friend, enemy.
CLOUD: Clud, rock, hill; symbol of divine presence: indicates the splendor it conceals.
CLOWN: Chump, peanut.
COFFIN: Abolitionist basket; the horny environment of a horse's hoof.
CORPORATION: Invisible body granted recognition as a separate entity (cloud) having its own rights and privileges; potbelly.
DEAD: Lacking elasticity or bounce; marked or doomed (see Hubba Roc, Glossary 2); a programming failure or crash; not broadcasting; dust entrainment and deposition; destruction of enemy air defense (see Zero, Glossary 7).
DEATH: Act of dying; volant intercourse; don't ever antagonize the horn.
ENLIST: To list, as from a rope; to enumerate, make lists; to frob; to make lists.

FROBNICATE: "To frob a frob;" to manipulate, tweak, or twiddle; connotes aimless or gross manipulation; fine-tuning.
GENERAL GOODWRENCH: Friend of Conway during the noumenal operation, ontic general manipulator of the wers machine, reputed master programmer capable of tweaking or twiddling, capable of frobbing; "trust your vehicle to General Goodwrench."
HYSTERICAL: Of the womb, believed that hysterics ensue when lifted above its place.
LIFE : See Game of Life, Glossary 2.
MOB: Refers to enemy, any computer-controlled creature or motile object.
MUMBLE/MUMBLAGE: Topic of mumbling; stands in for obscenities; used when a better response is too complicated, as in "well, mumble."
OBSCURE: Implies a total lack of comprehensibility, "the reason is obscure" means the problem could theoretically be articulated, but it is not worth the effort.
PENDULOUS: Hanging, dependent, as on a rope or ligament (religioned).
PROCREATOR: Professional spawner of soldiers and dogs; procreators work on the highest low ropes just below the actual battles; without them we would not have wer.
RECREATION: Variant of procreation, the spawning of new programming.
RELIGION: To bind together, tie fast.
TODDLER: Clown spawned on holidays by General Goodwrench, so called due to its difficulty balancing.
UNIFORM: An intermediate language developed for reverse engineering.
WER: Wers: to confuse, mix up; werza: confusion; wurst: sausage; term for recreation that involves religion (battle).

Glossary 2: Part 2

BARK: Telling everybody what you own.

BATTLE: To compete on bungee cords or tightropes using blades or boffers (see rap).
BLOW UP: To become famous or fully understood; to make sense; to parse.
BLOW UP THE SPOT: To expose; to expostulate.
BOFFER: Foam weapon used against a child; check for sharp or abrasive surfaces and make sure the layers are not too heavy; users should protect the eyes.
BOMB: An impressive thing, person, or event; a piece of fruit.
BOMBARD: Compound bomb/bard; *synonym: knocker, doorknocker.*
BIT BUCKET: Mythical destination of deleted or inaccessible data.
BREAK: To cause to be broken; "your latest patch broke the server;" to pause and examine for intersection of bugs; "If a bug stops you have an intersection, and that is always a breakpoint."
BRILLIANT BUZZARD: Suspected 2STO Launcher/XB-70 Aircraft, aka Blue Eyes.
BUGLE RAG: U2 Photo Update RBS Sit-Chart Production.
CONWAY: Inventor of the game of life, as well as sprouts, philosopher's football, the soma cube, and the still unsolved angel problem; inventor of the *surreal numbers.*
DOG: Best friend, partner; the opposite of god fallen under the earth.
DON JAUN: A completely finished negative operation.
FLAME: To speak incessantly.
FOO: Fubar, generally a name for any living thing.
FOODOG: Compound foo/dog; edible antichrist
FOO FIGHTER: Unidentified flying object, phooey; fighter being flamed.
GAME OF LIFE, THE: A cellular automaton invented by Conway, it is the best-known example of a cellular automaton; the game has attracted interest because it is an example of emergence and organization. Life has a number of recognized patterns, and several interesting examples include the evolving

F-pentomino (pentimento), the self-propelling glider (Jason), and various guns that can be used to generate a stream. For many aficionados, life is simply a programming challenge, but for some it means more. Actually a zero-player game, life's evolution is determined by its initial state, needing no input from players. It runs on a grid of cells that stretches to infinity, each cell in one of two states: either alive or dead (on/off).

GOSPER: Holder of a place of pride in the lisp community, the hacking forefather; noted for his work on continued fraction representations of real numbers and for closed-form hypergeomatric identities; became interested in the game of life shortly after Conway proposed it; Conway conjectured the existence of infinitely growing patterns and offered a reward; Gosper found a pattern and won the prize. He is also the inventor of the ontic hashlife-algorithm originator originator, which can speed up life by many orders of magnitude (see God, Glossary 6).

GUN: To forcibly terminate a program or job; blammo; a device consisting of a cathode ray tube, which emits electrons, and a surrounding electrostatic apparatus that focuses and accelerates electrons; Gunilda, woman's name applied to a siege engine.

HOMEBOY: A close male friend, dog.

HOMELAND: Birthplace of the original peanut; a volant place for making weapons and learning to walk ropes; located beyond the sky.

JIFFY: Interval of time, commonly 1 millisecond; an indeterminate period of time from seconds to forever; to say "I'll do it in a jiffy" means certainly not now, possibly never.

KILL: To cease operating; keep prospecting, instill prospecting, live prospecting, love prospecting; to deliver a blow hard enough to disable the helm, in some places regarded as an open-faced Norman helm, in others as a closed pot helm.

LISP: Designed to process lists or enlistment, widely used in artificial intelligence.

MEASURING TAPE, THE: Good for structure; by wrapping it around the face, you may become intimate with the structure of the face. Chalk and a measuring tape combined with small blackboards serve as a nighttime mirror of dark flashes, creating a motion picture that mimics human life throughout the night, allowing for prosthetic emotions to be worn as a tangible disguise.
OUTLAW SHARK: UFN Classified Surveillance/C3I Program.
PEANUT: Pendulous chump; person to be dealt with in a jiffy.
POGO: A highly extensible, skinnable, and configurable program launcher with controls including rotation, shifting, and switchable views.
RAP: To knock on wood (flame, mumble, rave).
RAPPER: Soldier engaged in rapper sword dancing, spirit rapper.
REAL: Retaliate for every attack line, pendulous defense against opposing funambulists.
RAPPER SWORD DANCING: Tightrope dancing with courtesy swords: soldiers and priests swat with flexible strips of steel: one stationary, one fitted with a swivel.
RAVE: To speak authoritatively on a subject about which one knows little (flame).
SCA: Society for creative anachronism, pronounced "ess see ay" or "scah," scadians.
SKILL: Variant of kill, weapons a scadian is capable of using, such as wearing a hat.
SMOKING CLOVER: Psychedelic color munch due to Gosper.
SPIRIT RAPPER : One who claims to receive messages from the dead.
TICK: Interval of time (jiffy), discrete unit between iterations; often left unspecified since the only constraint is that *caused things happen after causes.*
TRACTOR DUMP: UF Army Classified Tactical RDT&E, aka Tractor Bat, Tractor Dirt, Tractor Flop, Tractor Hole, Red.

WORD: Exclamation, as in "yes, I agree;" question, as in "oh word?"

Glossary 3: Part 3, Section A

BELTED FIGHTER: Flying soldier/priest who delivers volant sermons during battles.
BIBLE: Authoritative manual for lisp operating system (chine nual).
BOUNCE: To make an exit or leave the premises without a tangible door.
BUBBLE: A dog or bubble that has become a scrub; a type of transportation.
BUBBLE DANCER: OpOrd U2 Worldwide Weather Sampling.
BUSTED JAW: Aka Cobra Jaws, Rivet Jaws, Rivet Neck, Nancy Rae, Lisa Ann, modified under Big Safari.
BUSY LAWYER, THE: U2 Reception Plan for VIPs.
CHICKENHEAD: A procreator enlisted into battle.
CAPTAIN SAVE-A-HOE: Soldier seeking attention from a chickenhead, but who always ends up bouncing alone.
CHINE NUAL: Lisp machine manual, so called because the title is wrapped around the cover so that only those letters show (see Bible).
COBRA JUDY: Ship-Based Radar System TELINT Missile Test Surveillance AN/SPQ-11 On-Board Observation Island Stationary in Pacific; aka Cobra Shoe.
COLLEGE GIRLS: High-Level Intercept Activity U2.
COLLEGE MAIDEN: Strip Chart Recorder AN/FPS-17(XW-3) Detection Radar.
COMBAT MARTIN: F-105Fs Carrying QRC-128 VHF Jammers for MiGs Block.
CREW: An organized group of doorknockers.
GARBAGE COLLECTION: System of automatic memory management that reclaims memory used by objects that will never be referenced again; when a system has a garbage collector it is usually part of the run-time and said to be garbage collected.

HARVEST REAPER: Development F-111 to Make Combat Ready.

HAYSTACK: RB-50G ELINT Configured Aircraft 44 RB-50Bs.

HEAD DANCER: 3 EC-135K ECK '55-3118' ECK '59-1518' '62-3536' JEB.

HEAD: Person, mug; seat of reason (dome); person considered foolish (chowderhead, chickenhead); device in tape drive that enables the reading of data on prosthetic face; hand-held encryption authentication device.

HITTING SKINS: Volant intercourse (see Death, Glossary 1).

HOME: Start position, beginning of a line; to a target automatically.

HOMESLICE: A silent dog (buckminster).

HUBBA ROC: A peanut marked for the kill (shelled).

IDEALIST: CIA U2 Codename Development, aka Little Face.

LITTLE BROTHER: Study to Equip Cessna Model 337 Super Skymaster.

LONG LEGS: Aka Operation Long Thrust, College Girls, College Maiden.

MACK MURDERER: Enemy player who hates game (pluffer).

OFFICE BOY: 3 RC-135D '60-0356' '60-0357' '60-0362' aka Lucky Boy.

PRIEST: Belted fighter; programmer.

SACRED: Reserved for exclusive use: "Accumulator 7 is sacred to the UUO handler;" anyone may look at a sacred object, but clobbering it will screw up what it's sacred to.

SCHEME: Dialect of lisp developed by Steele, clobbered by Gosper and Sussman; unashamedly minimalist, it's goal is not to pile feature upon feature, but to remove weaknesses and restrictions that make new features appear necessary. Scheme uses lexical variable scoping to support explicit continuations; it supports garbage collection; originally called schemer in the tradition of planner and conniver.

SCRATCH: Scrilla, paper, mail, ends, lucci, cabbage, stacking, bolshevik.
SCRUB: A worthless peanut.
SERMON: Tedious program; flame offered as reproof or exhortation in pendulous flight.
SUSTAIN HOPE: Operation UN/NATO Coincided with Shining Hope.
SUSSMAN: Known for his contributions to artificial intelligence, including debugging and propagation of constraints, as well as dependency-based explanation and backtracking. Using digital orrery and Jack Wisdom, Sussman discovered evidence for the chaotic motions of the outer planets.
TACIT RAINBOW: Northrop AGM-136A Anti-Radar MissileUAV.
VOLANT EYE: Hurricane Tracker WC-130; flying spherical camera that transmits battle.
WILD WEASEL: UFAF SEAD Program F-100-F BECKLES.
WISDOM, JACK: Author of "Chaotic Lagrangian Trajectories Around an Elliptical Vortex Patch Embedded in a Constant and Uniform Background Shear Flow."
WRITER: Graffiti artist, spirit rapper; rapping soldier (jock, chub).

Glossary 4: Part 3, Section B

BAGBITER: A program that fails (bags); "This bagbiting system won't let me get out of spacewar;" *synonyms: cretinous, bletcherous, chomping.*
BARF: Term of disgust (bletch), to choke, as on input: barfulous, barfitious.
BEEF: Disagreement or conflict, combat beef.
BIT: Information from yes-or-no questions; when seeing someone you haven't talked to for a while, it's common for one or both to say, "I have a bit set for you."
BITE: To steal another's ideas, lyrics, style (byter, bagbiter).
BLETCH: Disgusting in design or function, bletcherous.

BOOTIE CRACK CORN: A variety of peck feed; bad, phony.
BROCCOLI: Marijuana.
BYTE: Component in data hierarchy usually larger than a bit but smaller than a word.
CHEWY: Marijuana laced with cocaine.
CHOMP: To lose; to chew on more than one has bitten; a hand gesture consisting of four broken fingers held together like a mitten, meaning, "chomp chomp."
CHONG: Marijuana laced with crack cocaine.
CHOPPING IT UP: Having a conversation; rapping, flaming.
CHOP SUEY: A Chinese AK.
CLEAN: Extremely tight, dipped in butter.
COLD CHUCK: To throw meat on a table or grill (chunk); OpOrd RB-57F.
COMBAT APPLE: Aka Burning Candy, PACAF OpOrd RC-135M Rivet Cord.
COMBAT BEEF: Build-up of Strategical Reserve TAC units (Beef Broth).
COMPASS COOKIE: Data Guideline SAM Drones Fang Song.
CORN: A gold tooth.
COTTON CANDY: OpOrd KC-135A-II RC-135D, aka Office Boy and Rivet Stand.
CRUNCH: To reduce the size of a file by a complicated scheme unrelated to the original data, such as a huffman code: the file ends up looking like paper crunched into a wad; # *sharp number hash pig-pen mesh crunch*; aka octothorpe.
CUBAN CANDY: OpOrd Burning Candy.
DAEMON: A dormant server that waits for certain conditions to occur, such as the appearance of a stray goose.
DUCK: Female Gander, modified under Big Chief.
ELIGIBLE RECEIVER: DOD Testing Vulnerability of Infrastructure to Cyber Attack.
FEAST GEAR: Scoupers, troughs, beef buckets, plates, gobble garb, grill funnels, chomp suits, crunch gloves, gorge helmets, food tents, nosh sleeves, long teeth, etc.

FEASTOCRAT: Prandial officer responsible for preparatory feasts.
FAKE ICE: Good for treating wounds; identical fake cubes are often found beneath a soldier's second tongue.
FLAM ARTIST: Culinary torch chief (brandy blazer, liquor lighter, farm boy).
FIERY RELIEF: Delivery of Supplies to Volcano 353 BURT SOG MAC-30.
FISH: Action on bungee cord, to offer oneself as bait (yu-shiang whole fish); another metasyntactic variable (foo) having no specific characteristics.
FISH BOWL: Operation Fish Hook.
FISH HOOK: Operation Fish Bowl.
FLAKEY: Operation subject to frequent lossage.
FLAVOR: Flava; variety, type; on lisp machine, class of object.
FLAVORFUL: Aesthetically pleasing, *antonyms: random, losing.*
FLUSH: To delete something, to abort an output operation.
FRIED: Not-working due to hardware failure (crispy).
FROG: Anything (foo, fish); of people, somewhere between a turkey and a peanut toad.
FRUIT: Explosive weapon (combat apple).
FUDGE FACTOR: Parameter varied ad hoc, producing the desired result. The terms "tolerance" and "slop" are also used.
GARLIC SALT: Sub-version of Rivet Stand, KC-135A '55-3121' '59-1465' '59-1514' modified under Big Safari.
GAS: Extermination; "Some loser just reloaded the system for no reason! Gas!"
GERMAN CHOCOLATE CAKE: A kilo of A-1 yola.
GOBBLE: To obtain or consume (snarfle).
GORP: Another metasyntactic variable, good old raisins and peanuts.
GRAVY: Grave (bunce), contents of a coffin, combat juice.
GRILL: A person's face; his gold corns or gridiron; bubble mouth.

GRIND: To format lisp code by indenting so it looks pretty; hence, "pretty print;" to run interminably tedious tasks, crunch (see Treadmilling, Glossary 6).
GRONK: To clear the state of a wedged device, more severe than "to frob;" of people to go home and sleep; gronk out.
HAVE DONUT: MiG-21F-13 Air Combat Training at Groom Lake, aka Have Idea, Have Garden, Have Nap, Have Orator, Have Stork, Have Void, Judy Blue.)
HOE CAKE: Flapjack; someone who does not receive the respect of his peers.
JUICE/JUICING: Respect; having good hydraulics.
LICKING OFF: Short for licking off shots, firing, flooding mugs.
MARINATING: Relaxing; bleeding to death.
MASHING: Moving or driving quickly; diving without a cord.
MONEY/MONEY HOLE: Brother, dog; gun (mouthpiece); bluff blinker.
MOUTHPIECE: Flame hole, rapper hole (have orator); coffin; corn chamber; gun.
MUNCH: To transform in serial fashion, requiring large amounts of computation.
PEACE PHEASANT: FMS Program, aka Peace Patch, Peace Pharaoh, Peace Dragon.
PELICAN: Order of great merit, membership granted by the Crown; the insignia is of a pelican in her piety, wounding her breast to feed her nestlings.
PIGEON: Object of special concern; wounded soldier.
PILOT FISH: UFN Tactical RDT Program.
SERVE/SERVER: To defeat an opponent; daemon service for the requester; to be incarcerated; to sling fodder or kill.
SLOP: One-sided fudge factor, often to avoid a fencepost.
SLURP: To read a large data file into the core before working on it.
SNARF: To grab a large document or file without the author's permission.

STRAY GOOSE: OpOrd 4+ C-130E-I Combat Talon Leaflet Dropping, Orchestrated by Burning Hand, aka Bright Candy.
TASTE: In programs, quality that tends to be inversely proportional to the number of features, hacks, and kluges; also tasty: "this feature comes in N tasty flavors."
TONGUE: Bell clapper; a device for manipulating wurst.
VANILLA: Ordinary flavor, the standard; for example, "vanilla-flavored wonton soup," or simply, "vanilla wonton;" chong.
WATER PUMP: Operation Ho Chi Air Commando Interdiction.
YAK: Cognac; to talk persistently (chatter, flame).
YU-SHIANG WHOLE FISH: Character gamma used by lisp; tends to elicit incredulity from people who hear about it.

Glossary 5: Part 3, Section C

ARMS: Forelimbs, flippers; when set on fire, firearms (chong slingers).
BADGE: Identifying portion of the flipper; iron knuckle; base air defense ground environment/equipment.
BALDRIC: A wide ornamented belt worn over the shoulder; ribcage.
BAMA: Knocker in outdated costume who does not know how to bear arms; for example, a peanut who still wears a red shirt.
BELLS AND WHISTLES: Unnecessary but amusing features; nobody seems to know what distinguishes a bell from a whistle.
BOOTSIE: Bad, phony; made infamous by the Clicker.
BURNER: An edible telephone used during battle to blow things up.
BURNING PIPE: Aka Burning Candy, modified under Big Team.
CHIP: Thin slice of semiconducting material (homeslice); dried cow dung.
CHROME: Gun-Shaped Flashlight.
COMBAT ARROW: OpOrd UFAFE Combat Talon C-130E.

COMPASS: Communications planning assistant; computer-assisted surveillance system; computerized optimization model for predicting and analyzing support scenarios.
COMPASS BUFFALO: Reconnaisance drone, aka Busy Robot.
DESERT SHIELD: Aka Desert Storm, Desert Strike, Desert Thunder.
DOG TAGS: Used to identify foo fighters after a sun bath (see Sun Bath, Glossary 7).
DOME PIECE: Circlet, headdress, hair.
DRAGON: Program similar to a daemon, except that it is not invoked, but instead used to perform various secondary tasks, such as keeping track of unicorns.
DUCK HOOK: Combat Spear OpOrd Special Operation C-123.
DWIM: Do what I mean: able to guess what result was intended when provided with bogus input.
ELEGANT LADY: UFAF Classified Tactical Program.
FLAP: Floppy pocket; old hackers tell of the days when the disk was 0 and microtapes were 1 and 2: attempting to flap 0 would start a motor banging in a nearby cabinet.
FAVOR: Ribbon or small decorative laceration; given as a mark of esteem.
FIREARMS: Battle done with arms set aflame.
FLAMING DART: Operation OpOrd UFN Air Raids, aka Tapered Duck.
FLY: Frozen in flight, as a sortie into the upper atmosphere.
FOREST GREEN: SIGINT Intelligence Collection Operation.
FROB: Trunnion, protruding arm; by extension anything small.
GARB: Battle clothing, not including feast gear.
GOLD ONES: Components of the grill or corn chamber.
GRAVE: Appropriate to death (butter).
GUN-SHAPED FLASHLIGHT: Disorganizer of water (defibrillator), creating hysterical snowflakes that must be isolated when they reach the ground; priests return individual

snowflakes to their original fields of water, restoring order to the clouds.

HAIR: Complications; "DWIM is incredibly hairy;" sometimes hair is infinite, connoting terminal mud.

HAND: Flipper (emblem) connected to prosthetic arm (volant feather).

HAVE GOLD: NAIC Program Launch SVC AltAir Target Missiles (Minutemen) from C-130 ATSRDF, aka Have Donut, Have Void, Have Thought.

HEAVY CHAIN: OpOrd Clandestine, aka Thin Slice, Rivet Yard, Combat Sam.

HEAVY WEAPONS: Boffers exposed to high gravity.

HOOD: Dome protector; a particular part of the dome (Block Party); see Eric, Glossary 6.

HOOK: Extraneous software; a catchy beat or refrain; "off the hook" is very exciting.

HULA HOOP: Compass dome in which burner or faulty is effective in revolving transmission; mechanical propulsion via gyrating spiral tube; "slingatron."

JIMMY HAT: Conception blocker; worn by inspectors.

JOCK: A large, brute-force programmer.

LOGICAL: Not corresponding to reality; derived from "logical device" wherein a physical device is referred to arbitrarily; for example, suppose Les Earnest decided to leave and was replaced: the replacement would be the "logical Les Earnest."

LOOKING GLASS: Airborne National Command Post (ABNCP) to Maintain Command and Control After a Nuclear Attack, Based on EC-135E.

LOW GOOSE: A handed-down goose (stray).

MOON DUST: Coordination of Information on Decay/Deorbit of Space Debris.

SENIOR LANCE: U2R Goodyear Inflatable Dome.

SMELL ME: To understand (grok).

SMOP: Refers to programs that could obviously be written, but are not worth the trouble.

STEEL: Gat, chrome, flashlight, licker.
STUNNAS: Sunglasses.
TAG: Assigned to identify data in memory; "instead of signing with a cursive tag, Super Kool painted his name on the subway in huge block pink and yellow letters."
TIMS: Boots.
WOOFER DISGUISE: Hood characterized by dark bass (dog catcher, boomerang).

Glossary 6: Part 3, Section D

AGGRO: Daring and skillful; "an aggro mob will attack the non-cloaked ones."
AUTOCRAT: Individual in charge of wer; tyrant, implementer.
BOLD VENTURE: CTF Exercise New Horizons.
BRIAR PATCH: CIA-sponsored Sub-Version Rivet Stand, KC-135A / KC-135R (I) '55-3121' modified under Big Safari.
BRAIN-DAMAGED: "Honeywell brain damage," theoretical disease invented to explain certain cretinisms in Multics.
BRIGHT STAR: Exercise, joint with 11 nations including Jordan.
BUFFALO HUNTER: OpOrd AQM-34L/M Low-Altitude RPVs.
BUGGING OUT: To act crazy, to behave in an abnormal fashion.
BUBBLING: Rising up, coming about, bubbling under.
BURNING VISION: SAC OpOrd RC-135X, aka Cobra Eye.
BUZZ: To fly in a tight loop with no guarantee of straightening out.
CLOSE: Abbreviation for "close (or right) parenthesis" to eliminate ambiguity.
COBRA JAWS: Special teeth worn in battle: 1 KC-135T '55-3121.
COBRA MIST: Back-Scatter Over-the-Horizon Radar.
COMBAT ANGEL: Chaff-seeding, Ordnance Delivery Drone, AQM-34G/H/Q.

CORPSE: A collection of writings stored in a coffin (rap sheet).
CORPSE RUN: When a soldier dies he or she may leave a corpse. Participants fly back to it from pre-determined spawn locations to retrieve lost tags. A corpse run discourages reckless compiling and abuse of the death system.
DAY MODE: See Phase.
DRAMA: Trouble; excessive emoting or harping (Saga, see Glossary 7).
EMOTE: An action that allows soldiers to act out feelings or moods.
ERIC: The border of a field designated for combat; a petrified pun developed when the known world tourneyed together, marking fields with long strips of red cloth.
FARM: To repetitively gather resources; grinding.
FLOSSY: Showing off, flossing the golds.
GABRIEL: An unnecessary stalling tactic such as tying one's shoes; "pulling a Gabriel" or "Gabriel mode."
GOD: Opposite of dog; one step above an autocrat.
HANDWAVE: To gloss over a complex point or support it with blatantly faulty logic; "Boy, what a handwave!"
KILL ON SIGHT: To attack without provocation.
LIST: *Listen*: to desire, to please; designates the border of the field and by extension the field itself; *to list*, as from rope or ligament; *enlist*, volant; a special pointer, for example zero, marks the end of the list.
LOSSAGE: Result of a bug or malfunction, refers to corpses after a battle.
MAD: Mutual assured destruction.
MAGIC: As yet unexplained; "This routine magically computes the parity of an eight-bit byte in three instructions."
MARGINAL: Of small probability; "The power supply was marginal anyway, no wonder it crapped out."
MAVING: Named after a soldier in TinyMUD (see MUD, Glossary 7) who put a colon on the front of a whisper, causing

his private messages to be broadcast to the moon; applies to any confusion involving say, whisper, page, or pose.
MIKE NOVEMBER: Operator of the volant eye with Uniform Victor; replaced former operators Bravo Delta, Juliet Kilo, Lima Mike, Papa Quebec, and Romeo Sierra.
MISFEATURE: A feature that eventually screws one; it is not the same as a bug because fixing it involves a gross philosophical change.
MOON: Phase of the moon; to wander or pass time aimlessly; something unreasonable or unattainable; MPLS (multi-protocol label switching) Over OTN (optical transport network) network.
NINJA: Corpse capable of looting corpses; NORAD Integrated Node for Joint Assessment.
OUT OF POCKET: Excellent; very stupid.
OLD GRIND: Old battles (treadmilling); U2 Photography SAC ZI Bases.
PARSE: To translate or list, "It's very simple, you just kretch the glims and then aos the zotz;" a parsed fish means a fish deboned, although there is some controversy over whether "unparsed" should mean "bony" or "obscure."
PHASE: Waking/sleeping schedule; it is not uncommon to change one's phase by as much as six hours a day on a regular basis; "What's your phase?" / "I've been getting in about 8 PM lately, but I'm going to work around to the day schedule by Friday;" a person who is roughly 12 hours out of phase is said to be in night mode. To change phase the hard way is to stay awake. To change phase the easy way is to keep on sleeping.
PHASE OF THE MOON: Humorous random parameter: "This feature depends on having the channel open in mumble mode, having the foo switch set, and on the phase of the moon."
PLATFORM: Propel layer for availability, transactions, fragments, objects, relations, and messaging; specific combination, hardware, operating system, compiler, as in "this program has been ported to several platforms."

RAIN: Refers to a type of spell that affects an area of the game's geography and the soldiers caught in it (cloud, snowflake).
RANDOM: Undistinguished, incoherent.
RAPE: To screw violently, often used in describing file-system damage; "so-and-so was running a program that did absolute disk I/O and ended up raping the master directory."
REAL USER: Non-programmer; a deceased person, NPC.
ROLLBACK: The full state of the battle is usually not permanently saved, but at intervals; to fix an outcome unacceptable to god, the game may have to be rolled back.
SAMPLING: To obtain a urine sample.
SHEEPWALK: UF Classified Intelligence Program.
SUN BATH: Update-46-B52F-M117F Bombs Held Externally; the complete termination of a battle or wers programming schedule (see Zero, Glossary 7).
TENSE: Very efficient; highly bummed, but sometimes based on great ideas; a comment in a clever display routine by Kazar goes, "This routine is so tense it will bring tears to your eyes. Thank Gosling for inspiring this hack attack."
TREADMILL: Pejorative for grinding, bumming; "I'm close to hitting the 45 treadmill."
UNIFORM VICTOR: Cohort of Mike November, enemy of Xray Yankee Zulu.
VOLANT GHOST: Operator of volant eye; Meteorological Reconnaissance WC-130.
WEDGED: From "head wedged up ass," to be in a locked state incapable of proceeding without help; often refers to humans suffering misconceptions, "The swapper is wedged."
WHITE CLOUD: UFN Reconnaissance Surveillance Satellite (Cloud, see Glossary 1).
XRAY YANKEE ZULU: Operator of lifts transporting entertainers, priests, and rappers to the top of the dome; in spare time, enjoys golf, whiskey, echoes, and dancing the tango at the Hotel India; enemy of Uniform Victor.

Glossary 7: Part 3, Section E

BANGING: Really good, awe inspiring; an overzealous form of emoting.
BOGOSITY: The degree to which something is bogus, measured with a bogometer; "Handwave, my bogometer triggered."
BOLT: Damage skill that causes a projectile to fly towards an enemy; to leave, jet.
BOOM: Before object-oriented methods; slang for smoking clovers; typically used to catch floating logs.
BRILLIANT PEBBLES: SDIO Space-Based Laser/Recon, originally Big Bird; destroys all life inside a dome, producing snowflakes and a sun bath or zero.
BUCK WILD: Uncivilized behavior; doorknocking.
BUCKY BITS: Produced by META shifts, the idea came from Wirth, who commanded, "Burn all LEDs is a double-bucky F."
BUG: To cause a dog to start barking or wagging.
BUM: To make highly efficient or tense, often at the expense of clarity.
BURNING WIND: OpOrd RC-135V RC Rivet Joint.
CANONICAL: How a soldier is religioned, determining his swoop; vanilla.
CATATONIA: A wedged system; characterized by rigidity or extreme flexibility.
CHIRURGEON: Robot with medical training who sleeps during battles; only registered hackers of the Dome Guild or College of Chirurgeons are authorized.
CRASH: Often caused by a bug, a drastic failure.
CREDIBLE CHASE: 17 AU-23A Aircraft, aka Credible Sport.
DISCO LIGHT: A soldier's consciousness; IR Jammer AH-64.
EXCL: Abbreviation for ! (shriek, wow); when followed by QUEST, interrobang.
FEATURE: Unintentional feature; a bug can be changed to a feature by documenting it; sometimes called crocks, as in

"crash stoppage bug screw loss misfeature," or, "crock kluge hack win feature perfection."

FEEP: The bell of a display terminal, aka bleep; breedle is sometimes heard where the terminal bleepers are not particularly soft.

FENCEPOST ERROR: Discrete equivalent of boundary condition, often exhibited by iterative loops. "If you build a fence 100' long with posts ten feet apart, how many posts do you need?"

FINE: Good, but not good enough to be cuspy.

FLIPPER DROP: AFNS 981104, aka Dumbo Drop.

FLOW OFF: To keep moving and not stay in one place for too long (roll).

FREEDOM TRAIN: Myth of soldiers granted freedom at the end of a broadcast, refers to attendant sheepwalk; operation using tactical air sorties, usually followed by extended dumb-bomb aerial interdiction (Linebacker).

FUGAZI: Fouled up got ambushed zipped in; something fake; a deserter.

GETTING OVER: Succeeding, coming about (sometimes at the expense of others).

GLITCH: A sudden interruption or change in sanity or program function, sometimes recoverable (gritch).

HACK: A quick job that produces needed result; to cut or mutilate by hacking; "I hack x" is roughly equivalent to "x is my bag."

HACKER: Writer, rapper; someone who makes furniture.

HELLO WALL: Can you talk to a wall? (see Wall).

HOLD: Meaning "Stop whatever you're doing and freeze;" first learned by children.

LAMPING: Hanging out; marinating; producing juice.

LINE FEED: To feed paper through a terminal; to initiate a volant attack; the "character" that performs these actions.

LINE STARVE: To be cut or hacked from the air.

MUD: Real-time reality experiment descended from BartleMUD; newer versions include AberMUD and TinyMUD, as well as the cutting-edge Moo.

MURPH: Kill.
NERF: To intentionally weaken a skill or feature in the interest of balance, usually carried out by an Autocrat; "They're going to nerf priests in the next patch."
OFF THE HOOK: Great, said of a skillful maneuver on a bungee cord.
OUT THE FRAME: Away from the battle; outside the list or Eric; beyond the dome.
OPEN: "Open (or left) parenthesis" to eliminate ambiguity, one might say, "Open def-fun foo, open eks close, open, plus ekx one, close close."
PAVE PAWS: Phased Array Warning System Radar.
PEACE: Goodbye, farewell; later.
POP: Dialect pop-jay; based on procedure return instruction; to return from digression; "popj, popj" means roughly, "Now let's see here, where were we?"
PUNT: To give up, typically without any intention of retrying.
ROLL: To move or walk; "Puffy rolled out of the limo and into the party."
RUDE: Badly written; functionally poor, as in a program difficult to use due to gratuitously random design decisions.
SAGA: A cuspy (fine) but bogus raving dealing with N-random broken people.
SHRIEK: EXCL, bang, common among mathematicians!
SMART: Said of a program that does the right thing; there is a difference between calling a program smart and calling it intelligent; there do not exist any intelligent programs.
SMOKE: Sparse matrix operator kernel emissions; to kill with a gun (blammo); vaporous system made up of particles in outer space; to crash; blow up.
SNAFU: Situation normal all fucked up.
SPLAT: Circle-x character, also called blobby and frob; canonical for output routine that outputs whatever the local interpretation of splat is (nobody really agrees).
SPLATTERED: Splattered means shot.

STORY TELLER: P-3C C3I/SIGINT System.
SUITCASE RANGER: First Tactical Ruby Rangefinder.
SUN RUN: Modification Program RF-101C '56-0165' and Others.
SURPRISE PACKAGE: Modified under Pave Pronto.
SWOOP: Picking something up.
TAIL RECURSION: See Tail Recursion.
THRASH: To move wildly without accomplishing anything (swapping systems).
TRAP: Program interrupt caused by illegal action in user program.
VORTEX: SIGINT Satellite Previously Known as Chalet.
USER: A programmer who will believe anything you tell him, and who asks questions; identified with "loser" by the spelling "luser."
WALL: Shortened form of hello wall; an indication of werza, usually spoken with a quizzical tone, "Wall?"
WHEEL: A privileged bit that canonically allows the possessor to perform any operation on timeshare, such as logging others out of the system; "We need to find a wheel to unwedge the hung tape drives."
WHEEL WERS: Period during which wheels hack each other, delete files, or otherwise wreak havoc.
WOLFING: Yelling; swallowing food.
WOW: Bang!
YOYO MODE: State in which soldier bounces (see Phase).
ZERO: End of broadcast or program during which all remaining participants are splattered; death; sun bath; to erase or discard all data, said of directories where zeroing need not involve writing zeroes throughout the area being zeroed; having no measurable value; zoning and emotional range omitted; culmination of the game of life.

◆

Biographies & Acknowledgments

Rufo Quintavalle was born in London, studied at Oxford and the University of Iowa and now lives in Paris. He is the author of several books of poetry, the most recent of which, *hhereenow*, is published by corrupt press in Luxembourg. He used to run the reading series, Poets Live, has taught creative writing at NYU Paris and is lead actor and co-creator of the poetry and film project, *Coldhearts.* Rufo is an environmentalist with a particular interest in agroforestry and regenerative agriculture. He is a co-founder of Fruits of the Amazon, a company that grows organic fruit on degraded land in the Brazilian Amazon.

J. R. Solonche is the author of *Beautiful Day* (Deerbrook Editions), *Won't Be Long* (Deerbrook Editions), *Heart's Content* (Five Oaks Press), *Invisible* (nominated for the Pulitzer Prize by Five Oaks Press), *The Black Birch* (Kelsay Books), *I, Emily Dickinson & Other Found Poems*(Deerbrook Editions), *In Short Order* (Kelsay Books), *Tomorrow, Today & Yesterday* (Deerbrook Editions), *True Enough* (Dos Madres Press), *The Time of Your Life* (forthcoming April 2020 from Adelaide Books), *The Porch Poems* (forthcoming 2020 from Deerbrook Editions), and coauthor of *Peach Girl: Poems for a Chinese Daughter* (Grayson Books). He lives in the Hudson Valley.

Bryson Newhart has been published in many journals, including *Anemone Sidecar*, *Cafe Irreal*, *Caketrain*, *Elimae*, *Harp and Altar*, *No Colony*, *Tarpaulin Sky*, *Third Bed*, *Snow Monkey*, and others, most of which have gone out of print.